Vocabulary Workbook CURRICULUM

SOCIAL STUDIES • SCOTT FORESMAN • PEOPLE AND PLACES • SCOTT FORESMAN

PEARSON

Scott
Foresman

Editorial Offices: Glenview, Illinois • Parsippany, New Jersey • New York, New York
Sales Offices: Parsippany, New Jersey • Duluth, Georgia • Glenview, Illinois
Coppell, Texas • Ontario, California • Mesa, Arizona

www.sfsocialstudies.com

ISBN 0-328-09065-4

6 7 8 9 10 V011 12 11 10 09 08 07 06

© Scott Foresman 2

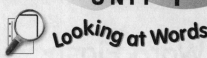
Clapping Game

Write each word on the lines under the number of parts you hear.

history	law	vote	rural
community	suburb	urban	capital

One Part

1. _____

2. _____

Two Parts

3. _____

4. _____

5. _____

Three Parts

6. _____

7. _____

Four Parts

8. _____

 Directions: Read the words in the box aloud with me. Clap once for each part of the word you hear. After we say each word, write the word under the number of parts you hear.

 Home Activity: Invite your child to play a clapping game to show how many parts there are in different words.

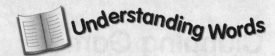

Word Flash

Play the word flash game with a partner. **Write rural, suburb,** or **urban** for each picture.

1.

_____

2.

_____

3.

_____

4.

_____

5.

_____

6.

_____

Name _____

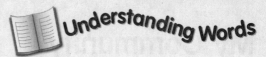
Understanding Words

Picture It

Write the word that completes each sentence. **Draw** a line from the sentence to the picture that matches.

1. I use my _____ to help choose a class trip.

a.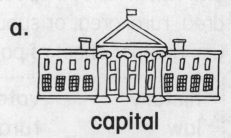

capital

2. I obey the _____ because it helps keep my neighborhood clean.

b.

vote

3. I live in a _____ with very different neighborhoods.

c.

law

4. I visit the _____ city of my state to see where the government works.

d.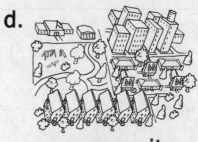

community

Directions: Write the word that correctly completes each sentence on the line. Then draw a line from each sentence to the picture and word that completes the sentence.

Home Activity: Play a word association game with your child using the vocabulary words on this page. Read one word to your child and ask him or her to say the first word that comes to mind.

My Community

Narrative Writing

Every community is special. Write to describe your community and what makes it special. Tell about what makes it an urban area, rural area, or suburb. Use vocabulary words. You may use another sheet of paper if needed.

history	vote	community	urban
law	rural	suburb	capital

_____

_____

_____

_____

_____

_____

_____

 Directions: Follow along as I read. Every community is special. Write to describe your community and what makes it special. Tell about what makes it an urban area, rural area, or suburb. Use vocabulary words. You may use another sheet of paper if needed.

 Home Activity: Look for pictures of communities in newspapers, magazines, and picture books. Ask your child whether the communities are rural, suburban, or urban. Discuss what things in the pictures give them clues.

© Scott Foresman 2

law

vote

community

A choice that gets counted. We <u>vote</u> for class president.

A rule that everyone must follow. Police officers help make sure the <u>law</u> is followed.

A place that is made up of many neighborhoods. There are many stores in my <u>community</u>.

UNIT 1

Vocabulary Workbook

history

urban

suburb

An area that has a city. We just moved to an urban area.

Tells the story of people and places from the past. Pictures of people can tell you about history.

A type of community that is located near a city. The suburb I live in is close to New York City.

✂

rural

capital

The city where the leaders of a state or country work. Washington, D.C., is the <u>capital</u> of the United States.

An area with small communities and open space. The farm is in a <u>rural</u> area.

One Who Does

If a word ends with a consonant, add **-er**:

> play + **-er** = player
> **Player** means "one who plays."

If a word ends with a silent **e,** drop the **e** and add **-er**:

> dance + **-er** = dancer
> **Dancer** means "one who dances."

Read these definitions. **Use** the suffix **-er** to write the words they define.

1. one who consumes _____

2. one who produces _____

3. one who farms _____

4. one who drives _____

5. one who sells _____

6. one who rides _____

7. one who bakes_____

8. one who uses _____

9. one who sings _____

 Directions: The suffix *-er* means "one who." You can add *-er* to an action word to make a new word. (Explain the examples to students.) Read each definition. Use *-er* to write the correct word for each definition.

 Home Activity: With your child, look through a storybook. Look for words with the *-er* suffix. Ask your child to name the base word to which the *-er* suffix was added and to explain its meaning.

Compound Words

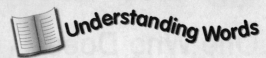 **Understanding Words**

Landform is made up of two words: land|form

A **landform** is a <u>form</u>, or shape, of <u>land</u>.
Draw a line to separate the words. **Write** your definition of each compound word.

1. grass|land

_____

2. hilltop

_____

_____

3. waterfall

_____

_____

4. seashore

_____

_____

 Directions: A **landform** is a form, or shape, of land. If you know the meanings of the words "land" and "form," you can guess the meaning of **landform**. Read each compound word. Look at each picture. Each compound word names a kind of **landform**. Write what you think each compound word means.

 Home Activity: Ask your child to combine these word pairs to make compound words: *water* and *way*, *river* and *bank*, *sea* and *side*, *coast* and *line*, *quick* and *sand*, and *main* and *land*. Help your child to predict the meaning of each compound word.

Name _____

Picture It!

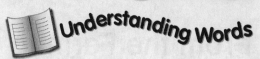

Draw an example of the vocabulary word in each sentence.
Write what you drew to complete each sentence.

1.

Wood is an example of
a **natural resource.**

2.

_____ is an
example of a **producer.**

3.

_____ is an
example of a **crop.**

4.

_____ is an
example of a **consumer.**

 Directions: Read the vocabulary word in each
incomplete sentence. Use your vocabulary
cards to find the meaning of each word. Think
of an example of each word and draw a picture
of it in the box. To explain your choice, write
what your picture shows on the blank line.

 Home Activity: Together with your child, look
around the area where you live. Point out
examples of **natural resources, crops,
producers,** and **consumers.**

From the Farm to You

Expository Writing

The food that we buy travels a long way to get from the farm to the store. Think about where the food we eat comes from. Then write to explain how fruits and vegetables get from the farm to a grocery store. Use vocabulary words. You may use another sheet of paper if needed.

geography	landform	conservation	crop
producer	consumer	natural resource	

_____

_____

_____

_____

_____

_____

_____

_____

 Directions: Follow along as I read. The food that we buy travels a long way to get from the farm to the store. Think about where the food we eat comes from. Then write to explain how fruits and vegetables get from the farm to a grocery store. Use vocabulary words. You may use another sheet of paper if needed.

 Home Activity: Look to see where food items or other items in your home come from. Discuss how these goods might travel from where they are made to you. Look up where these places are on a map.

geography

landform

ancestor

© Scott Foresman 2

Different shapes on the surface of the earth. A mountain is a kind of landform.

The study of the Earth and the ways people use it. The globe helps me learn about geography.

A person in my family who lived before I was born. My great-grandmother is my ancestor.

producer

consumer

natural resource

Someone who buys and uses goods. A consumer buys goods at the store.

Someone who makes or grows something. A farmer is a producer.

A useful material that comes from the earth. Soil is a natural resource.

✂

crop

conservation

The care and protection of land, water, plants, and animals. Park rangers teach people about <u>conservation</u>.

A kind of plant that people grow and use. Corn is a <u>crop</u> that provides food.

Singular and Plural

Write the words that mean one under <u>Singular</u>. **Change** them to mean more than one. **Write** the new words under <u>Plural</u>.

> income   goods   services
> tax   factory   trade

	Singular	**Plural**
1.	income	incomes
2.		
3.		
4.		

Write the words that mean more than one under <u>Plural</u>. **Change** them to mean one. **Write** the new words under <u>Singular</u>.

	Plural	**Singular**
5.		
6.		

 Directions: (Review with children the rules for making singular nouns plural.) *Top:* Write the singular nouns from the word box on the lines under "Singular." Write their plural forms under "Plural." *Bottom:* Write the plural nouns from the word box under "Plural." Write their singular forms under "Singular."

 Home Activity: Ask your child to explain to you how he or she figured out which words were singular and which words were plural.

Name _____

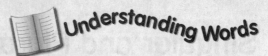

Make a Match

Draw lines to match the people with things they would **trade** for.

1.

a.

2.

b.

3.

c.

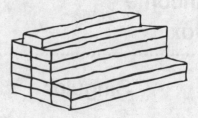

4.

d.

 Directions: Look at the pictures. Think about why people trade. Draw lines from the people to the things they would trade for.

 Home Activity: Help your child to understand trade by looking at labels of household items, such as clothing and electronic equipment, to find where each item was made.

Vocabulary Workbook

The Table Trade

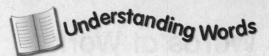

Write the word for each step in the correct order on the lines.

transportation
Ship the tables.

trade
Sell the tables.

factory
Make the tables.

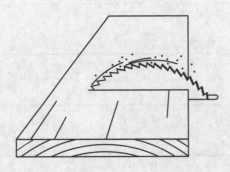

goods
Load the tables.

1. _____

2. _____

3. _____

4. _____

 Directions: Look at the pictures of the table trade. Think about the order of the steps. Write the word for each step in the correct order from first to last on the lines.

 Home Activity: Discuss with your child how a **factory, goods,** and **transportation** are related to retail trade and interstate trade.

Name _____

Words at Work

Narrative Writing

People must work and save money to buy things they want and
need. Think of a good or service you would like to buy. What
would you do to earn enough money to buy it? Write to explain
how you would work to earn money to buy a good or service.
Use vocabulary words. You may use another sheet of paper
if needed.

| income | goods | barter | services |
| factory | trade | transportation | |

_____

_____

_____

_____

_____

_____

 Directions: People must work and save
money to buy things they want and need.
Think of a good or service you would like to
buy. What would you do to earn enough
money to buy it? Write to explain how you
would work to earn money to buy a good or
service. Use vocabulary words. You may use
another sheet of paper if needed.

 Home Activity: Discuss with your child how
your family earns and saves money. Create
a savings plan with your child to help them
see how working and saving can help them
earn money.

Vocabulary Workbook

© Scott Foresman 2

income

goods

services

Things that people make or grow. Many kinds of goods are sold in stores.

Money that someone earns. Some of my family's income is used to buy shoes.

Jobs that people do to help others. A restaurant worker provides services.

UNIT 3

tax

factory

trade

A building where people produce or process goods. Juice is bottled in this <u>factory</u>.

Money that is collected by a government. Some of our <u>tax</u> money will be used to build a new school.

To buy, sell, or exchange goods. People can <u>trade</u> goods at a market.

transportation

barter

To trade goods or services for other goods or services without using money. People can <u>barter</u> to get what they need.

A way of moving goods or people from place to place. An airplane is one kind of <u>transportation</u>.

Which is Proper?

Circle the common or proper noun below each sentence that correctly fills in the blank.

1. I am a ___ of the United States.

   citizen   **Citizen**

2. My father was named ___ of the Week for his volunteer work in the schools.

   citizen   **Citizen**

3. The U.S. capital is named after ___ George Washington.

   president   **President**

4. Our school plans to elect a student ___.

   president   **President**

5. The Washington ___ opened in 1888.

   monument   **Monument**

6. Many towns build ___ to honor their soldiers.

   monuments   **Monuments**

7. A meeting was held between the ___ and the governor.

   mayor   **Mayor**

8. The key to the city was given by ___ Wilson.

   mayor   **Mayor**

 Directions: (Give examples of common nouns for a person, place, and thing and some proper noun counterparts on the board.) Circle the common noun or proper noun below each sentence that belongs in the blank.

 Home Activity: Look at a newspaper or magazine article with your child. Help him or her identify nouns as common or proper.

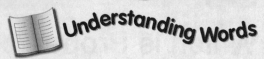

Leaders

Write the name of the leader. **Circle** the place.

mayor	governor	President

1. The _____ is

the leader of the

city.   state.   country.

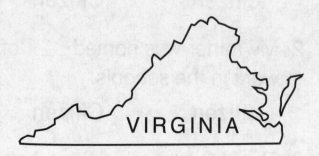

VIRGINIA

2. The _____ is

the leader of the

city.   state.   country.

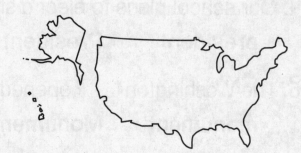

3. The _____ is

the leader of the

city.   state.   country.

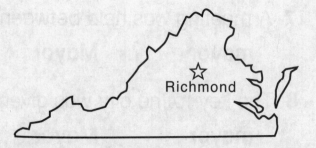

Richmond

 Directions: For each sentence, choose the name of the leader from the word box who leads the area shown on the map. Write the name on the line. Circle the type of place that leader is in charge of.

 Home Activity: Work with your child to identify related words that can be ordered from greatest to least. For example, family words: *grandparent, parent, child.*

Name _____

Word Help Wanted

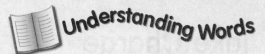

Understanding Words

Complete the "Help Wanted" ads below.

mayor	governor	President	Congress

Congress

WANTED: People who

will _____

_____

_____

governor

WANTED: Person who

can _____

_____

_____

mayor

WANTED: Person who is

ready to _____

_____

_____

President

WANTED: Someone who

can _____

_____

_____

 Directions: A "Help Wanted" ad is used to tell people about available jobs. Read the name of each job opening. Write a description of each job for each ad.

 Home Activity: Use a newspaper or other local resources to help your child find out the names of your mayor, governor, representative, senators, and President.

Take Charge

Narrative Writing

Town leaders have important jobs. They must make the community a place where people like to live. Suppose you could be mayor of your town. Write a speech to describe what you would do to make your town even better. Use vocabulary words. You may use another sheet of paper if needed.

government	**mayor**	**citizen**
governor	**Congress**	**President**
freedom	**motto**	**monument**

_____

_____

_____

_____

_____

_____

_____

 Directions: Follow along as I read. Town leaders have important jobs. They must make the community a place where people like to live. Suppose you could be mayor of your town. Write a speech to describe what you would do to make your town even better. Use vocabulary words. You may use another sheet of paper if needed.

 Home Activity: Discuss with your child the changes that were suggested in his or her letter. Explain how even everyday citizens can work to help improve the community. Together, learn about the different groups and organizations that work to improve your community.

government

mayor

citizen

The leader of a town or city. The <u>mayor</u> spoke at the town meeting.

A group of people who work together to run a city, state, or country. Our <u>government</u> makes laws to help keep us safe.

A member of a community, state, and country. I am a <u>citizen</u> of the United States.

governor

Congress

President

The part of a government that writes and votes on laws for all of our states. I hope to be elected to <u>Congress</u> someday.

The leader of a state's government. The <u>governor</u> came to our city.

The leader of our country. The <u>President</u> gave a speech.

freedom

motto

monument

A word or saying that people try to live by. A <u>motto</u> is written on this symbol.

Every citizen's right to make choices. The Liberty Bell is a symbol of <u>freedom</u>.

A building or statue that honors a person or event. The Lincoln Memorial is a famous <u>monument</u>.

Name _____

Looking at Words

Syllable Starter

Write each word on the lines for its number of syllables. Then **write** your own words.

| shelter | explorer | colonist | pioneer |
| tradition | colony | independence | |

Two Syllables

1. _____   2. _____

3. _____   4. _____

5. _____   6. _____

Three Syllables

7. _____   8. _____

9. _____   10. _____

11. _____   12. _____

Four Syllables

13. _____   14. _____

15. _____   16. _____

 Directions: Count the number of syllables in each word in the box. Write each word under the number of syllables it has. Then write words of your own that have two, three, and four syllables.

 Home Activity: Invite your child to play a clapping game to show how many parts there are in different words.

Name _____

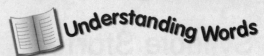

Related Pairs

Draw lines to match the related words.

1. colony   teaching

2. singing   free

3. teach   **colonist**

4. producer   sing

5. freedom   produced

Write the word from each pair that completes each sentence.

6. The _____ helped to <u>colonize</u> the new land.

7. The <u>freed</u> bird enjoyed its _____.

8. She is _____ in a group that <u>sings</u> in the schools.

9. The <u>teacher</u> enjoys _____ second graders.

10. The <u>product</u> was _____ in the factory.

 Directions: *Top:* Draw lines to match the related pairs of words. *Bottom:* Read the sentences. Choose the correct word from each matched pair to complete each sentence. The underlined word in each sentence is a hint to which pair to choose from. Write the word on the line.

 Home Activity: Have your child list some household chores. Challenge your child to write two related words for each chore. For example: *wash—washing—washer.*

Name _____

Clue Groups

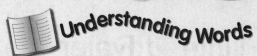

Understanding Words

Write the word that is described by each group of words.

1. _____

discoverer

travel

new places

2. _____

person

comes from another country

ruled by another country

3. _____

holidays

family events

done again and again

4. _____

place

settled by new people

belongs to another

5. _____

free

do it myself

on my own

6. _____

go west

settlers

wagons

7. _____

house

cabin

building

 Directions: Draw a vocabulary card. Look at the groups of words on this page. Find the group that lists things that go with the word on the card. Then write the word at the top of the group. Keep going until all the vocabulary cards are used.

 Home Activity: Help your child use the clues on this page to make up riddles about the vocabulary words.

Time Traveler

Expository Writing

You learned about three different time periods in our history. Suppose you could travel back in time to one of these time periods. Think about what life was like for early Native Americans, colonists, or pioneers. Then, write a journal entry to explain what your day was like in one of these time periods. Use vocabulary words. You may use another sheet of paper if needed.

shelter	**explorer**	**colonist**	**pioneer**
tradition	**colony**	**independence**	

_____

_____

_____

_____

_____

 Directions: Follow along as I read. You learned about three different time periods in our history. Suppose you could travel back in time to one of these time periods. Think about what life was like for early Native Americans, colonists, or pioneers. Then, write a journal entry to describe what your day was like in one of these time periods. Use vocabulary words. You may use another sheet of paper if needed.

 Home Activity: Discuss why it is important to remember the important events and people that make our country what it is today. Together with your child, come up with a list of important holidays, monuments, or other symbols we use to help us remember our history.

shelter

tradition

explorer

Something that is done a certain way for many years. Celebrating Independence Day is a family <u>tradition</u>.

A place where people live. People need <u>shelter</u>.

A person who travels to a new place to learn about it. Meriwether Lewis was an <u>explorer</u>.

colony

colonist

A person who lives in a colony. A <u>colonist</u> in Jamestown had to work hard.

A place that is settled by people from another country. Virginia was an English <u>colony</u>.

independence

pioneer

A person who goes first and prepares the way for others. A <u>pioneer</u> needed to work very hard.

To be free from other people or places. The colonists wanted <u>independence</u> from England.

ABC Order

Write the words in ABC order.

drum   doll   deep

1. _____ 2. _____ 3. _____

tool   tape   think

4. _____ 5. _____ 6. _____

Write the words from the word box in ABC order.

> immigrant   holiday   custom   landmark
> artifact   invention communication

1. _____

2. _____

3. _____

4. _____

5. _____

6. _____

7. _____

 Directions: When words begin with the same letter, look at the second letter in each word. Put the words in the ABC order of the second letters. *Top:* Write the words from each group in ABC order. *Bottom:* Write the words from the word box in ABC order.

 Home Activity: Look together at a dictionary. Find the guide words, the two words at the top of each page that tell the first and last word on the page. Help your child look up each word from the word box in the dictionary.

© Scott Foresman 2

Compound Words

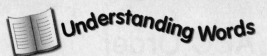

Write each compound word. **Write** the meaning of the compound word on the lines.

1.

land + mark = _____

_____

_____

2.

water + fall = _____

_____

_____

3.

black + board = _____

_____

_____

 Directions: Each pair of words makes one compound word. Look at the pictures and the words. Write each compound word on the line. Write a definition for each compound word on the lines that follow.

Home Activity: Have your child identify the household objects and places, such as a cookbook or bedroom, whose names are compound words.

Name _____

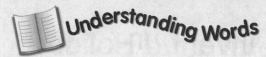

Get the Meaning?

Write what the picture shows to complete each sentence.
Circle the correct meaning of the underlined word.

| clock tower | compass | grandfather | museum |

1. My _____ was an **immigrant**.

    Immigrant means

    a person who settles in a new country.

    a person who builds a new home.

2. The _____ is a **landmark** in our town.

    Landmark means

    an important place.

    a government building.

3. We saw an African **artifact** in the _____.

    Artifact means

    a tool for fixing something.

    an object made and used by people.

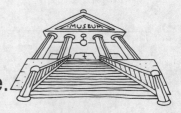

4. The _____ was a Chinese **invention**.

    Invention means

    a game or toy.

    something new that someone makes or thinks of.

 Directions: Compare the pictures to the words at the top of the page. Write one of the words on the lines to complete each sentence. Circle the meaning of the underlined word.

 Home Activity: Say the vocabulary words to your child. Have her or him say the definitions of the words.

Invent a Holiday

Narrative Writing

Holidays are an important way we remember special people and events. Think of something you feel should be celebrated with a holiday. Write to explain why your new holiday is important and how it would be celebrated. Use vocabulary words. You may use another sheet of paper if needed.

immigrant	holiday	custom	landmark
artifact	invention	communication	

_____

_____

_____

_____

_____

_____

_____

 Directions: Holidays are an important way we remember special people and events. Think of something you feel should be celebrated with a holiday. Write to explain why your new holiday is important and how it would be celebrated. Use vocabulary words. You may use another sheet of paper if needed.

 Home Activity: Ask your child what holidays he or she enjoys. Together, discuss why these holidays are important.

immigrant

holiday

custom

A special day. Our
favorite holiday is
Thanksgiving Day.

A person who settles
in a new country. My
grandfather was an
immigrant to our country.

A special way that a
group does something.
It is a custom to celebrate
some holidays by having
a parade.

✂

landmark

artifact

An object made and used by people. We can learn about the past when we look at an <u>artifact</u>.

A building or place that is important or interesting. Mount Rushmore is a <u>landmark</u>.

invention

communication

Sharing ideas and information with others. The telephone is used for <u>communication</u>.

Something new that someone makes or thinks of. The wheelbarrow is an <u>invention</u> many people use.

CURRICULUM